The history behind science and the science that makes history in healthcare business

Preparo de originais:	*Diagramação:*	*Capa:*
Gabrielle Antunes	Cintia Rodrigues	Ygor Moretti

A editora não se responsabiliza pelo conteúdo da obra, formulada exclusivamente pelo(s) autor(es). A editora não se responsabiliza pela manutenção, atualização e idioma dos sites referidos pelos autores nesta obra. 1a Edição, 2024 — Edição revisada conforme o Acordo Ortográfico da Língua Portuguesa de 2009. Publique seu livro com a Ases da Literatura. Para mais informações envie um e-mail para originais@asesdaliteratura.com.br.
Suporte técnico: A obra é comercializada da forma em que está, sem direito a suporte técnico ou orientação pessoal/exclusiva ao leitor.

Catalogação na publicação
Elaborada por Bibliotecária Jéssica Carraro - CRB-14/004/24

E83h

Etges, Ana Paula Beck da Silva

_The history behind science and the science that makes history in healthcare business / Ana Paula Beck da Silva Etges. – Rio de Janeiro: Ases da Literatura, 2024.

104 p.; i.; 14 X 21 cm

Ilustração da capa: Valentina Frasson Torino.

Texto em inglês.

ISBN 978-65-5428-714-2

1. História da Ciência. 2. Gestão em Saúde. 3. Economia e Organizações de Saúde. I. Título.

CDD 509.2

Índice para catálogo sistemático
I. História da Ciência

ANA PAULA BECK DA SILVA ETGES

The history behind science and the science that makes history in healthcare business

*To my parents, Roberto and Sandra,
and my husband, Ricardo.
Who are my earth, and exactly for this
reason, allow my mind to fly.*

*To my nephews and godchildren,
Valentina, Lorenzo, Afonso, and Aurora:
never stop studying and learning, always having
your purpose as humans with you.
In the Era of machines, wisdom
keeps our souls alive.*

Summary

Acknowledgments

Thank you to all the leaders behind the histories shared in this book: Prof Carisi Polanczyk, Prof. Robert Kaplan, Dr. Tomas H Lee, Prof. Richard Urman, Prof. Nadine Clausell, Prof. Sheila Martins, Mrs. Anne Gebeulle, Dr. Junaid Nabi, Dr. Porter Jones, Dr. Ana Claudia de Souza, and Dr. Rafael Vargas. Your role in this field is strongly contributing to build a better healthcare system, inspire and educate gritty future leaders.

Thank you very much to Bel Pesce. Bel inspired me and followed me during the book-writing process. My old dream about writing a book only became true with your support, motivation, and inspiration. The experiences, intelligence, and kindness you share with those who have the privilege to meet you move gritty individuals' dreams and purpose, which results in advances in people's journeys, increased business, and, consequently, innovation for society.

And especially, thank you very much to Carisi Polanczyk not only as a Leader behind the histories shared in this Book; Carisi is a senior mind and huge heart behind most of the histories shared, and who has been moved together with me through PEV Consulting, by the cause to transform healthcare systems to a value-driven perspective through science. There are no doubts about the future impactful histories we and PEV will account for together and potentially share in the future how close we will arrive to the history we wish to tell in 10 years. Thank you very much. This book would not have been possible without our partnership and friendship over the last few years – and counting-.

Opinion

"Ana Paula has an impressive mix of abilities and experiences that allows her to connect information and translate complex understandings in a unique manner, explaining both the historical as well as the visionary contexts in practical and relevant ways.

The book "The History Behind Science and the Science That Makes History in Healthcare Business" analyzes the various aspects and facts that influence what can be decisive in healthcare-related decisions, and it goes much further by showing extra parameters that are part of this complicated equation and by proposing inclusive and prosperous paths to a segment that needs constant reinvention."

BEL PESCE

Preface

Over the decades, healthcare systems have struggled to offer care and technologies to bring health to people while maintaining financial balance across institutions. This is a challenge, and data have shown that if we do not redesign the systems, several of them will collapse. In this environment, multidisciplinary professionals have been working to illuminate this path. This publication, " **The history behind science and the science that makes history in healthcare business,**" aims to provide a contemporary and provocative view of this dynamic area.

The motivation for this publication came from a rapid pace of innovation in health management and costing, value-based healthcare concepts, and the need to share personal and close colleagues' projects that integrate scientific research with practical applications. This book is intended to serve as a valuable reference for healthcare leaders and professionals, researchers, and students who are eager to understand, discuss, and bring these innovations into their practice.

The development of this publication was idealized and executed by Ana Paula Etges, a brilliant young engineer who happens to be provoked by the mess and non-sense organization of healthcare during her PhD in the USA. Fortunately for me, we crossed paths more than 7 years ago in collaborative research projects. Since then, we have been working together on several independent but interrelated studies aiming to provide scientific elements that could help improve the way healthcare is delivered in Brazil and other countries. In several of these projects, we teamed with leading experts in economics, statisticians, epidemiologists, data analytics, healthcare managers, and clinical physicians, who made parts of this work possible. Nonetheless, Ana Paula's intense, obstinate, and always ahead-of-time mind transformed our projects into a reflexive book about health management, cost containment, crisis management, and skills that health leaders must have.

The book is organized into four main sections: Leadership and strategic transformations; Cost assessment; Risk management and governance; and Creating a culture of valuable histories. Each section is based on real cases coordinated mostly by Ana Paula and me, providing readers with a holistic understanding of the problems in healthcare and, sometimes, how simple solutions could be applied. The last part is Ana Paula talking about the story everyone would like to hear if the changes occur shortly. A must-read segment.

I am sure that this publication will not only inform but also inspire further research and innovation in healthcare management and the sciences related to that, ultimately leading to improved patient care and outcomes.

My sincere compliments to Ana Paula, and to others who also contributed to this work. I am sure is the first of several, and probably sooner than 10 years from now.

CARISI ANNE POLANCZYK

The purpose of this book

This book is written by a scientist passionate about inspiring people with scientific education to build more effective, population-based healthcare systems. It is written by someone who believes that we can find answers to society's problems in science and assumes that the generations are changing faster than ever. It is written by someone who believes that histories educate, and people stop and get inspired by others' histories. As a scientist, it is written by someone with a history to tell behind each scientific development process already achieved.

With this in mind, this book will make people feel themselves in the history behind each scientific advance in the health policy, leadership, value, and economics fields, which are exposed to several non-answered questions and impact every individual alive on the earth. The healthcare systems worldwide are suffering, and there are thousands of projects, scientific developments, and incentives to transform how health services are delivered, paid, and managed. The transformation is necessary because of the consensus to create strategic models to manage organizations and policies to the systems driven to increase populational health and not exclusively focused on delivering healthcare services. It seems to be a simple word game, but it means modifying almost all the processes and agreements that make the healthcare system happen.

However, the scientific rigor required to publish and disseminate the social science advances in the healthcare business is extensive and, sometimes, can be hard to understand by those who are dealing with the challenges in the board of health organizations, including hospitals, payers, insurers, startups, and the state. The quick modification happening worldwide in how people get informed and interested in new content, innovative solutions, and potential strategies to guide themselves in implementing strategic transformations challenges us -as scientists- to innovate our communication activities and find ways to touch people's emotions and learning capabilities. Telling histories behind the scientific advances to demonstrate how science can accelerate the process to transform the healthcare system is the purpose of this book, which joined histories of strategy, leadership, cost and risk management and assessment, to explain how those are essential advances to create sustainable health policies and, consequently, valuable healthcare systems.

Leadership and strategic transformations in healthcare histories

Undoubtedly, great advances in how systems are structured have behind strong leaders: people who inspire and make teams work efficiently and aligned with the same purpose. As a common characteristic, those leaders are gritty, which is very well defined by Dr. Angela Duckworth[1] and means: people who combine passion and perseverance in all long-term goals and daily activities to achieve them; they do not give up and put effort into doing the right things, aiming to achieve the best impact. If we strive to redesign care services delivery, payment agreements, and how people deal with their health, identifying strong and gritty leadership is the foundation of those processes. Considering the technical and clinical aspects of any healthcare modification, it is necessary to account for people who naturally have clinical leadership and are persevering enough to collaborate with visionary, gritty executives.

The concept of value in healthcare emerged with the publication of the seminal article by Prof. Michael

Porter, "What is Value in Healthcare Care" [2] and with the Book signed by him and Prof. Elizabeth Teisberg "Redefining Health Care: Creating Value-based Competition on Results.[3] It happened in 2006-2010, and since then, several companies, researchers, and policymakers have searched for manners to make it happen. Among them, Prof. Tom Lee assumed an important position in disseminating the concept across oceans and bringing the importance of prioritizing the theme in discussions involving clinicians, policymakers, business managers, and the general society. As a consequence of these initiatives, the question of "How to redefine" a system that represents one of the central budget proportions of any country worldwide has been the focus of several scientific discussions and Forums, including the Global Economic Forum, which since 2020 added this topic as a central theme.

The history behind the LEADER Framework reports how redesign and value-based projects are being co-created and developed for a few clinical conditions. It tries to put together a structured sequence of domains for starting the journey of changing internal cultures to align several stakeholders to the same purpose without compromising anyone's financial sustainability.

The LEADER Framework

The LEADER [4] framework was developed to impact populational health by guiding structural and strategic projects in healthcare. The minds behind the LEADER are also behind most of the histories that will be shared in this book: Dr. Carisi Polanczyk, a senior leader behind impactful health policy projects that are shared along with the following pages, Dr. Junaid Nabi, who is a recognized global health policy scientist, and myself, who learned a lot from both of them and, sometimes, put them on the wall to think outside the box to create innovative solutions.

After years of working on strategic and scientific-based projects in healthcare, the creation history behind this framework is summarized: "introducing an easy-to-be-remembered, followed and implemented by medical and non-medical managers who are working to redefine care systems worldwide to create social impact, by increasing population health." Along with a sequence of discussions, the acronym L-E-A-D-E-R emerged:

L – Leadership and Care Integration

E – Effective Agreement

A – Accurate Outcomes Data

D – Data Measurement

E – Evaluation of Impact

R – Risk Mitigation

The theory of value in healthcare and the experience in implementing strategic and transformational initiatives in this business environment was the heart of the introduction of this easy-to-be-remembered and followed acronym. As international health policy scientists, during the process of consolidating the LEADER, we agreed that developing those projects in healthcare requires the participation of multiple stakeholders, and because of that, establishing a SHARED Leadership is extremely important. It is how we can deal with conflict of interest and maintain the purpose of all initiatives to improve population health.

In the real world of projects, making it happen involves using **E**ffective agreements and standardized **E**valuation processes to confirm that what is being developed is impacting healthcare access, efficient use of resources, and increasing value to society. This is how we can mitigate the **R**isk of driving new strategies in healthcare only for the financial sustainability of part of the stakeholders and not for the MAIN purpose of healthcare organizations, which may have individuals' health as the central goal. With the technological advances we have today, achieving that is only feasible by using **A**ccurate real-world and real-time **D**ata that represents specific care pathways and patients' conditions.

The LEADER Framework

Source: adapted from [4]

The LEADER framework has served as the background for several strategic projects, and we believe it can help several teams lead impactful healthcare value-driven projects worldwide. A few examples are in the fields of oncological, stroke, and chronic diseases.

LEADER for Redesigning oncological care pathways

It was the end of 2019 when a colleague oncologist who had just finished his Ph.D in cost assessment, Dr. Rafael Vargas, called me to share an idea. At the time, he was starting to serve as a local leader of an international committee focused on improving cancer care. Consequently, he was very motivated to start a project that had implications for the south of Brazil. It was known, but not measured, that the time for people to start a radiotherapy treatment after diagnosis was much longer than the expected period of 60 days established by the law in Brazil. Also, the primary bottlenecks behind this problem still needed to be identified. The project emerged with this purpose: measuring, pointing out the holdups, and, most importantly, joining local leadership to suggest what can be done to change this history.

We got involved in the three main reference centers and started to design care pathways to identify where the care was not integrated. Students and researchers were involved in observing and understanding the sequence of activities that patients submitted in each center and measuring the length of time in and between each activity. It was quantified that the patients were, on average, waiting almost one year to start the treatment, and most of the bottlenecks were explained, but the non-integration between primary care and specialized care, which do not use the same technological system. In the second part of the study, patients were interviewed, allowing us to point out challenges in communication with the patients who demonstrated difficulties, for example, in knowing the radiotherapy session being submitted and how many additional they had. With all these learnings and new information consolidated, healthcare leaders, clinicians, patients, and health technology assessment researchers were invited to participate in a co-creation process workshop to list what could be done to change this negative context. The result was a matrix of strategies that could be implemented and the identification of their implications in the system's procedures, systems, or communication with patients. The prioritization considered the impact on the patient's experience and the feasibility of implementing each strategy.

Strategies to improve the history of radiotherapy access in the South of Brazil

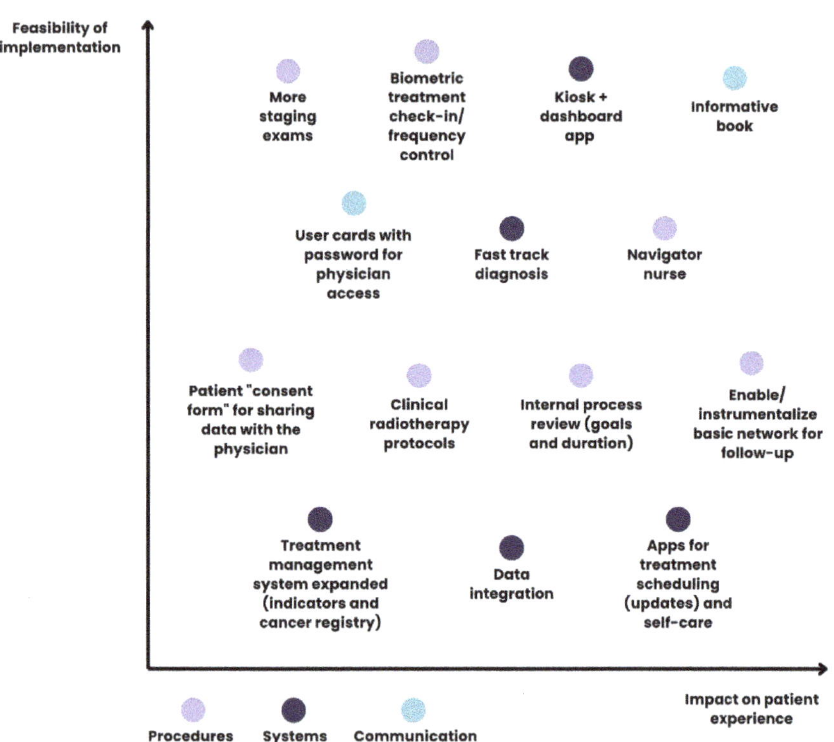

Source: Adapted from Etges et al. (2023).[5]

Summarizing the implications of using LEADER in this process, it is possible to highlight the following:

- Since the first phone call, the project has involved local leadership and the primary reference centers in analyzing care integration, and their participation was essential to identifying potential contributions to be implemented in each center.

- The size of the problem was measured and reported to policymakers.

- It was notified of the necessity to change agreements and invest in more technology capacities to proactively use data and improve care delivery.

- It pointed out what could be done to change history and redefine radiotherapy delivery in south Brazil.

LEADER for driving Stroke care pathways to value

The stroke field concentrates excellent efforts and investments in healthcare. While a lot of advances in technology are registered, cardiovascular diseases keep concentrating around 30% of deaths in Brazil, which is equivalent to 400,000 people yearly. This fact motivated our group to study and adapt the theory behind Value-based health care to the Brazilian perspective. To start the initiative with the participation of the essential stakeholders, the idea was presented to the National Stroke Networking (*Rede Brasil AVC*) in 2019 leader, Dr. Sheila Martins, who immediately supported the project. With their approval, 3 reference centers, 1 pos-doctoral, 1 Ph.D, and 4 master's students were initially involved in the project, allowing to account for the expertise of 4 senior professors from Medical and Engineering Schools. The research aspect behind this project allowed us to access financial resources from public funding in Brazil.

The multidisciplinary initiative had one main goal: *to improve managers' and clinicians' capabilities to manage the stroke care pathway supported by real-world data and structure the technology necessary to introduce value-based reimbursement agreements for stroke in the country.* Making it happen started by understanding the stroke care pathways established in each center, defining the standard set of measures that should be used to monitor the proper outcomes in the stroke field, and, very importantly, the intelligence necessary to automate cost monitoring started to be designed. Once all metrics were defined, standardized instruments were used to guide the data collection in each center. Monthly meetings were performed with each center to confirm that the data collection was advancing well. An essential difference in the development process behind this project was the continuous work of people with different expertise. The neurologist participated in all the project steps, bringing their requirement as clinicians and guiding that the algorithms correctly consider all the critical clinical variables. After six months of data collection in each center, the leading group of researchers could use the datasets collected and the value analyses to compare outcomes and costs across centers, technologies, and clinical risk consolidated. At this moment, the challenge of consolidating the analyses that will allow the study's primary purpose to be answered was on the researchers' table.

The challenges were then with the research senior group, which discussed the following questions: What are the main contributions and messages we can offer to society from this extensive project? After some sessions, it was a consensus that first, it would be necessary to publish the clinical validation of the model; once we have it, developing an intelligent and digital platform that the centers could use to automate the value analysis could facilitate its dissemination and also contribute to the National Stroke Network's guide to its use.

The first part was more accessible for the group because it is more usual in research: consolidating the results in a robust scientific paper and analysis. As a pioneering analysis, it was presented as a validation of a model to estimate stroke costs adjusted by the technology, patients' risk, and patients' outcomes, making it possible to use it to establish risk-sharing agreements between payers and providers. This is the most significant innovation of this study and represents an elementary step for payers and providers to align fair value-based contracts.[6]

The second part has a tone of integrating scientists and the market. Because of that, it is also a milestone in how academics and the software industry can work together to address the market requirements better. Identifying the request from the National Stroke Networking for a user-friendly solution to automate the value analysis, the research group worked in collaboration with a software development company. A co-creation process was followed during the development and design phases, contributing to making the solution more adjusted to the specific requirements of the neurologists and managers. The final output is a Business Intelligence Platform that allows the identification of benchmarks of care between hospitals and compares outcomes across therapies and patients' risk levels. The dashboard can be consulted online (https://webavc.prologica.pt/). [7]

The entire project was developed in 2 years, having direct implications by following the LEADER domains:

- The consolidation of how to evaluate value in stroke.

- Introducing a tool that can automate the hospital process to analyze value.

- It measured the variability in costs due to therapies, patients' clinical risk, and outcomes. This information is essential to guide any modification in reimbursement strategies used in the healthcare system and to establish fair agreements between payers and providers.

- It served as a starting point for several other health economics and value studies in the stroke field, including the extension of similar projects to eight different countries in Latin America.

- Integrating the right leaders from the clinical and policy aspects, along with developing this study, was extremely important for the project to achieve its goal of contributing to improving the system's capability to manage the stroke care pathway better.

- Integrating scientists and software development companies to introduce applied solutions to support healthcare services management processes is a landmark.

LEADER for co-creating and integrating care services

The principles of value in health include the establishment of Integrated Practical Units (IPUs), which have the principle to center care on patients' needs and integrate all the services required for each clinical condition. With the background developed in several previous projects and the scientific results published, other challenges started to emerge and made us look for answers in science. Among them is the continuous search for manners to integrate care processes, aiming to increase patient experience and outcomes and reduce waste.

Rare conditions, asthma and cardiovascular diseases were already the focus of those projects, where independently of the clinical condition, it is known since the early stage that the success of those initiatives requires the involvement of multiple stakeholders, strong leadership, and the definition of clinical protocols based on evidence and effective data collection and analysis technology. Identifying ways to put all stakeholders on the same page and develop long-term sustainable programs, involving the right people, defining agreements, and data governance to create new ways of delivering services are means to change organizational cultures and processes. It supports the creation of more effective and integrated manners to provide services to the population. It is expected that over the next years, it will be possible to measure the implications of implementing these strategies on improving health outcomes and reducing waste. Measuring the impact of those projects over time is how it is possible to identify what is working or not and scale the best strategies to several organizations, contributing to achieving more expressive results from a system perspective.

With the focus on integrating care, In Spain, a project that started in 2019, the HOPE Program,[8] is an excellent example of consolidating a complete, successful history in a short time. Following a similar sequence of steps, based on strong leadership, effective agreements, measuring accurate data, and integrating care, they redesigned the oncological service at the hospital. It resulted in an increase of 200% in patient access to the service, a reduction of costs by 24%, and a 25% in hospital readmissions, among other positive implications. The researchers report successful elements are the engagement of most clinicians, the use of digital solutions that facilitate the communication process with patients and providers, and the integration of care. In addition, measuring positive results and communicating them with the group helped develop TRUST and a continuous cycle of motivation for the project.

Humans naturally like to know that we are doing something better and progressing. Once these transformational projects are proposed, standardizing the measurement and communication processes is also a manner to develop a positive sense of competitiveness. Frameworks such as LEADER help guide the steps necessary to conduct those projects. Still, in all those strategic initiatives, after setting the primary goal as the implications on population health with financial accountability, exploring human natural behaviors is an innovative and effective way to achieve impactful outcomes and successful histories. Healthy competitiveness is undoubtedly one of these characteristics. It can serve as a trigger to engage professionals in creating a history of a more valuable, effective, and sustainable healthcare system.

Cost assessment in healthcare histories

Thinking about costs in healthcare is always a challenge; a straightforward explanation is that we quickly have access to charges, taxes, price information... But to answer how much a health service costs, always as the first answer it will be posted: "It depends." It depends on the perspective; it depends on what you consider as the hospitalization (for example, it includes previous exams and the consultation after discharge); it depends on the organizational focus (public or private system). So, something that is the first aspect that financial managers look for in any other market to establish accurate processes and systems in healthcare is always and anywhere a huge challenge.

The challenge starts with the way in which the system is structured. Most countries have healthcare expenses as a priority, which concentrates an expressive proportion of the government's budget. Independently of policy ideology, healthcare is always a central focus of national societal programs and needs to be. From the public perspective, the amount comes from taxes. In private organizations, the most usual way to access it is by contracting health insurance, which is frequently offered by companies to employees. In all these situations, we, as individuals, are paying a fee to expect to receive the treatment we need in the future. Once we use the service, we wish that we will be able to access public or private institutions and receive the specific and most advanced treatment or preventive care according to our requirements. The institution (hospital, clinic, healthcare center,...) never knows what patient is arriving, with what clinical condition, and with each payment condition each individual will offer, but has as a purpose to deliver the best care possible to each individual.

Payers, state or private insurers, usually pay providers for services delivered with a determined and standardized fee regardless of the variability due to clinical conditions or the outcomes achieved; the payment is, in general, standardized and known by all. This reimbursement strategy is called "Fee-for-Service," and it could not receive a better name. It is exactly what happens: patients are submitted to a specific service, and the organization is paid.

So, what is wrong with that, and why does it contribute to the system's sustainability since we do not really know the cost information?

Let's use the simple example of a blood count exam in an outpatient clinic. The first patient is elderly, with locomotion difficulty and a long history of previous disease. On the day, it is being investigated his reaction to the current group of medications that he is being submitted. The second patient is a middle-aged adult without a history of disease who is doing his annual check-up. Both arrive at 7 am at the clinic. The adult leaves the clinic in 15 minutes, happy that they can access all the results online until the end of the day. The elder left the clinic in 60 minutes, nervous about the results, and said they would return the next day to take the printed results. Both patients have the same insurance coverage and will pay an equal fee to the clinic. Our question now is:

Is the cost of delivering the same blood count exam equal to both patients?

It depends.

- **For the payer:** Yes, the exact fee will be paid for each patient.

- **For the patient:** directly, yes, both are paying their monthly fee to the insurer and have access to the clinic. However, the elder will spend more on transportation and own time to go to the clinic on the two following days.

- **For the clinic:** NO. The resources required to deliver effective care to older people are higher than for this specific middle-aged adult, and it is the clinic's problem to manage its resources to assist both. However, most clinics do not know how much this difference is and manage their financial resources based on the payment received.

In this simple example, we expose the problem: the healthcare system knows the fees but needs to accurately measure the costs of delivering care; consequently, it is always a challenge to answer whether a fee agreed upon is fair.

Another simple demonstration of how a payment system that do not accurately consider the cost information can strongly influence healthcare services availability and sustainability is in the orthopedic surgery field. High-complexity patients can require much longer hospitalization and resource consumption than low-complexity patients. If payers are reimbursing the provider with a unique fee for the same surgery, it naturally results in providers searching for at least a balance in the proportion of low-risk patients because the margin will be much more favorable than in the case of high-risk patients.

When Value-based Health Care was introduced in 2007, Prof Porter identified this unknown cost information problem and pointed out that one of the first things that had to change to redesign the healthcare system should be how payments were made. A better understanding of costs, not payments, is required to make this happen.[9] This was the moment when one of the most recognized Professors of cost assessment joined the journey of redefining healthcare, Prof. Kaplan, who validated the Activity-based Costing and Time-driven

Activity-based Costing models. This last one is already recognized as a gold standard for assessing healthcare costs. The reason for this is simple: the method guides the process to measure resource consumption along with a process or a care pathway, allowing the measurement of variabilities of each individual based on the length of time each individual spent in each activity. By applying this method, it will be possible to make factual cost information available, and then, more accurate payment models and financial management processes can be established.

In parallel, in the United Kingdom, strong research was conducted in the development of microcosting [10], which also intends to accurately measure costs at a patient level and use that information to sustain economic models, which are frequently based on secondary data. It means that it is common to guide decision-making processes in healthcare with cost data from analysis developed in other countries and adjusted by the national currency and inflation. It is acceptable in the health economy, and sometimes, it is possible to have a model -which is better than nothing, but the scarce access to local cost information can expose payers and providers to substantial financial risks.

My involvement in this field emerged for this reason. I was a cost assessment professor at the Engineering School and a Ph.D student at the time, attending a traditional health economics class at the University. During one class, the senior professor explained to me for the first time this problem about accessing cost information and how it was well acceptable to use payment fees as cost data for subside economic models. It instigated me as never in my professional journey so far. As a young Ph.D student, I put priority on bringing more from the engineering school to health economics and trying to do something to minimize this problem. Creating a Consortium of people to improve the quality of cost information will be one strategy.

The history of the TDABC Consortium

How can people from different expertise get together and work to have more qualified financial information used to sustain healthcare decisions? This was the question behind the origin of the TDABC Consortium. As health economics and policy scientists, creating solid structures and groups that can offer answers to policymakers and organizational leaders is society's responsibility. With this in mind, the consortium was born: a group of people with experience in developing microcosting, mainly using TDABC, sharing knowledge, challenges, and experiences aligned with the same purpose: to generate solutions for the global problem of measuring costs accurately.

The idea was introduced by a faculty member from Harvard Medical School, Prof Richard Urman, who became a great partner in developing methodological studies in the cost assessment for surgical pathways fields. The Brazilian group of researchers assumed the leadership to make it happen. After a few months, the consortium website was available online (www.tdab-cconsortium.com), joining researchers from several countries and consolidating a community of people working and innovating in how to measure costs. The first in-person meeting happened in 2021 in Lisbon, Portugal, and promoted a better integration of international groups. Among the strategic definitions of the meeting was to join efforts to standardize and improve the cost analysis in heart failure [11], which is the focus of part of the histories that will be shared here.

Nowadays, once a group starts a project, the communication channel on the network is frequently used to match groups working in similar fields, and merging knowledge can increase the impact of their histories. Chronic, rare, and infectious, ..., diseases integrate the examples of impactful projects developed.

The studies in the heart failure field

Cardiovascular diseases are responsible for approximately 30% of deaths worldwide, and heart failure is one of the chronic diseases that affect 64 million people around the world, being accountable for a huge burden and, consequently, a priority of the healthcare systems. The complexity of the disease can be figured out in very different manners when treating and monitoring patients. From a total outpatient and drug-based behavior to being submitted to very innovative and expensive technologies, such as artificial heart, heart failure concentrates a challenge to have cost data standardized to be evaluated. However, its economic impact deserves efforts from health economic scientists.

The history of heart failure microcosting analysis from the Consortium funders started with the support of the Ministry of Health in Brazil, which was considering incorporating extracorporeal membrane oxygenation (ECMO) into the national public healthcare system in 2018. Once this study started, it was recognized that better assessing the cost of heart transplants in the country was important. Then, one significant project emerged: the microcosting analysis of Heart Transplants in Brazil. At the time, the unique information was the reimbursement value the Brazilian government paid for hospitals: R$ 37,000 (around US $8,000 – in 2024). However, it is implicit that the actual cost for the care of patients submitted to transplants is much higher, but how much higher? It was only an impression without foundations- before the development of this first study in the heart advanced failure field.

To solve this gap, the Heart Transplant Cost project started. As the previous histories reported, it accounted for senior leadership from the faculty and the hospital leadership, Dr. Nadine Clausell. A group of cardiologists and health economists designed the strategy to collect and analyze the data, and in a few months, the first study reporting real-world cost data about heart transplants was published in the Journal of Cardiac Failure. The results consolidated only the hospitalization period of heart transplantation and already demonstrated that, on average, the total amount was US\$ 74,000.[12] Remember that the standard fee paid by the state is US\$ 8,000. Here, we have one more example of the risk of managing financial hospital resources and guiding decision-making processes considering fees instead of costs.

The paper's publication allowed the dissemination of previously unknown information and elucidated the importance of accurate cost analysis in cardiology. Influenced by that, several other projects emerged, and over the years, *only academic and research in collaboration with other groups made public the information regarding the cost of heart failure in Brazil.*

Ph.D students evaluated the outpatient and hospital-day costs in a multicenter project, telemedicine services to support patients, and studies for evaluating advanced heart failure submitted to Left Ventricular Assist Devices and palliative care were also developed with the support of private companies. From 2018 to 2024, it is already possible to report that, on average, the annual cost per patients who follow an outpatient behavior varies from US\$200 to US\$700 due to its clinical condition (more or less complexity).[13] For patients with a prior hospitalization for decompensated heart failure, US\$ 1,000, and for patients on a palliative care condition, US\$80,000. This information, bit by bit, has been documented and shared across academics, policymakers, and, very importantly, a society to change the history of providing access to adequate care for heart failure patients in Brazil.

The studies in rare disease

Rare diseases concentrate a great effort and expressive budget of pharmaceutical Research and Development Studies and are also responsible for part of the current challenges of healthcare systems sustainability. By dealing with particular conditions, the investment to achieve efficacious technologies are high, and the target population is always small, which results in expensive technologies to be evaluated and incorporated. In addition to this context, patients under these conditions are usually assisted in reference centers with very specialized and, frequently, multidisciplinary teams. These structures also have decades of research and investments in their background. Another point of the rare disease environment is the societal aspect. Families with rare disease members adjust their lives to assist the carrier individual. Frequently, parents leave their jobs to dedicate themselves to supporting a child with all the required care. Caregivers are hired to help manage the disease when it is possible. These facts exemplify the indirect costs that are not measured and are unknown by society.

It brings us to the point that adds purpose to several histories of health economics analysis in this field: We all agree that the drug's financial impact is expressive. However, is it alone? Or should we consider all the care chains required to effectively deliver care to those patients and families throughout their lives?

Blinded by the drugs' millionaire impact, the evaluation is expected to focus on the budget and resource distribution in the rare disease field, which is focused exclusively on medications and does not involve the extensive care chain fundamental to guarantee effective care delivery.

A sequence of scientific initiatives to measure this unknown information has emerged, targeting to change this history. From 2020 to 2024, hemophilia, Duchenne dystrophy, and spinal muscular atrophy concentrated efforts on impactful microcosting studies conducted using primary data in Brazil. The challenges, opportunities, and impacts learned while developing those projects give us the background to share a few insightful histories.

It was December 2019, the eve of the summer holidays, when I received a phone call from an HTA manager from a Big Pharma. The question was straightforward: Could a microcosting study be conducted for Spinal Muscular Atrophy in 2 months? My first answer was, why two months? When I listened to her answer, my passion for research in this field was touched: "It is the length of time we have to generate scientific evidence for the health technology incorporation process".

As scientists working in this field, keeping your purpose as a researcher and avoiding any ethical issues or bias risks in the invitations received is extremely important. In this case, for example, everybody knows that the industry is interested in incorporating expensive technology into the Brazilian public system. Still, the purpose was that the policymakers' decision needed to be as fair as possible, and considering the technology available today, if we do not measure this cost information, the analysis delivered will not strictly demonstrate the real world of those patients and families. With this in mind, our research group spent the summer working on the case.

A group involving health economists, clinicians, and nurses with experience in the disease was formed to start running the data collection as soon as the IRB was approved. My previous experience in developing microcosting projects was essential to receiving quick approval from the local IRB and following the research protocol. In February, the first analyses were presented to the sponsor on the days close to the carnival in Brazil.[14] A few days later, the meeting happened with the agency, and we were informed that the microcosting study added positively supported the decision-making process to incorporate the technology in the evaluation for a specific group of patients. In this case, our mission was achieved, and science impacted history.

What we could not imagine was the implications of this first landmark for other rare diseases: the news about the impact of measuring accurate cost information of rare diseases to subside essential definitions to the healthcare system ran fast across the country, and in a few months, several people from market access, patients' society, and technology agencies recognized the value of that. Here resides an essential part of this history: *communicating.*

Unlike other fields, the contributions achieved for rare diseases were strongly disseminated in forums with clinicians, patients' society, policymakers and academics, and other media such as webinars and social media. It resulted in a much faster dissemination of the value of better measuring costs and outcomes of care pathways and, consequently, accelerated information dissemination. From the scientist's perspective, work on those approaches also demanded another kind of preparation. Writing or speaking for peers is our everyday activity, but touching other audiences requires other communication methods. This issue was a legacy from the rare disease's projects so far: To make innovative information be used to change histories in healthcare delivery, it is necessary to use the channels that those who need to access the information already use. With the modifications in how people communicate and all the social media available, each day more is scientists' responsibility to be creative and effective in communicating with each specific audience.

The learning process effectively communicates the impact of the Spinal Muscular Atrophy study; in a few months, similar projects emerged for Duchenne[15] and Hemophilia.[16] Both of them had the same purpose: to generate accurate cost information about people living with those conditions to subside health technology evaluation processes under the public health system in Brazil. The cycle was repeated: in the rare disease field, adopting alternative communication strategies was triggered to amplify the impact of the new scientific-based information provided in rare diseases' economic history.

Another field that required effective communication was COVID-19.

The COVID-19 pandemic

I believe that any healthcare researcher worldwide felt the pressure and the necessity to contribute something when the pandemic started. Obviously, economic studies were not the first focus of research questions with more rush for scientific answers. Still, we knew that as soon as the clinical answers started to be disseminated, how to provide access and pay for them would be a question for all policymakers.

During the first home office weeks in the South of Brazil in March 2020, our national research group was in a meeting to define studies we will search for funding to develop. Measuring costs associated with the treatment was a clear requirement from the State. At that time, hospitals were being paid fees similar to those for influenza. However, the actual cost of the COVID-19 hospital and outpatient treatments was a white page. With the background in other clinical fields and the parallel amplification we were receiving on rare diseases, the request to assume the leadership of the cost assessment project was posted to us. I remember as if it was today that the group and I were a little resistant, maybe afraid, with all the uncertainty involved. Then, the Professor who knew me pretty well was my post-doctoral supervisor, and who has shared the coordination of most of these challenges reported in this book with me, used the 'magic' words to motivate the group: *"We know that we do it with high accuracy and strictly following validated methodologies, and we know the importance of this information to the society; if we do not do, someone will. And we do not know who someone will be."* It was enough to decide to submit the project to IRB and start.

Our first initiative was to evaluate the impact of the pandemic on hospital's financial structures. In early 2021, we published, in a peer-reviewed journal, an article reporting information comparing data between 2019 and 2020 in 10 Brazilian hospitals. We demonstrated, for example, that the hospitals, on average, lost 10% monthly revenue and that the ventilator acquisition costs varied from Int$ 17,000 to Int$ 48,000 without a justified technical reason behind this variability.[17] In parallel, the main study in Brazil aimed to determine the costs per COVID-19 patient, which was in development. Understanding the challenge and importance of this information worldwide, one more time, we accounted for support from the Professor from Harvard who is behind introducing the TDABC method and collaborated on the Consortium creation, Prof. Bob Kaplan. He accepts our invitation to support the project methodologically.

It was a multicenter, national level, microcosting analysis for a condition with (at the time) unknown variability in the care pathways. Also, during the study, the treatment protocols changed several times due to the context of the pandemic and discoveries. In practice, medications that at the beginning were being prescribed, at the end, were not anymore. I will say that we saw 'almost' everything on the COVID-19 raw data. As an engineer, finding consumption standards and care for the data was more difficult than ever.

Nevertheless, we did not give up; the first cost results were published in early 2023, reporting a mean cost per patient of around Int$ 6,000 but with variability from Int$2,000 to Int$17,000 comparing patients with only emergency hospitalization registered with those with only intensive care units' registers.[18] This information is necessary to estimate the real burden of the pandemic from the country's perspective. Until today, we are working on the final data analysis that will, finally, report the most accurate COVID-19 cost analyses based on primary data in Brazil and one of the most extensive studies with this level of granularity worldwide.

After 4 years of working on this highly challenging project, it has taught us several lessons:

#1 It is much more complicated and complex to develop economic studies for conditions where the clinical evidence is not consolidated and disseminated. The COVID-19 study demonstrated this several times, and in future similar situations that we hope will not happen with this intensity, we could wait a few more months to develop more robust projects.

#2 To find the right collaborations. Having international researchers' support helps achieve the required credibility to start the data collection with self-confidence. However, despite 10 centers participating in the first macro analysis, only five could finalize the data collection with credibility to join the final data analysis. Here is an essential lesson about dedicating reasonable efforts, in the beginning, to work with the institutions that have, in addition to the interest, the condition to join challenges such as this one and strong leadership to make it happen.

#3 The time necessary to develop the project with the required trust in data was longer than the length of time policymakers had to define policies. For example, we reported that the real-world cost is much higher than what was being paid by the fee-for-service reimbursement system; however, now that the information is validated and available, the payments already happened, and the volume of patients is small. Consequently, the results will serve much more to evaluate the burden of the pandemic for hospitals (which is essential to be reported) than guide definitions of sustainable policies, such as we were able to introduce for the Stroke field, for example.

#4 Solving the length of time problem can be done by incorporating technologies that allow for the collection of real-time resource consumption data. The good news is that this is already happening and available. In the next history, we will discuss the technological aspect further.

The digital technology advance and implications

Artificial Intelligence, digital technology explosion, telemedicine Era, ..., this is the real world we are living in. But how does it support policymakers' ability to manage healthcare systems better? This book has already shared several histories about strategy and cost assessment, reporting our challenges in generating accurate financial and outcome information to guide decisions. Is it possible to automate the data collection and analyses, making it scalable and faster?

The answer is that it is already happening but not disseminated, and the critical elements to making it happen are not easy to manage. Let's break the updated histories on this topic from two angles:

(a) automating financial and outcomes data from services based on digital technology, such as telemedicine and health apps (or electronic medical records)?

(b) implementing digital technologies to automate data collection and analysis in usual care services (such as surgical care pathways).

PART A:

COVID-19 was also a landmark in the explosion of digitalizing health and, in Brazil, the regulation of Telemedicine services. So, how much does it cost? What is the best strategy for defining payments for telemedicine? How does it contribute to the healthcare system? Is it easier to manage the resources and outcomes of telemedicine services? All those are very important questions that started to be posted with the advancement of innovative methods to assist patients.

Some answers:

- In general, the services start, and as usual care, the cost is not known;

- Each system and organization has defined its manner of paying for the service;

- Evaluate the service contribution. Universal healthcare systems with geographic heterogenicity, such as Brazil, can consider amplifying access to care, accelerating care lines, and sometimes resolution of cases, avoiding the necessity of patients going to specialized care.

And finally,

Yes, telemedicine services offer us very high-quality data that can be used to answer those questions and, in particular, manage the services in real-time. However, effective data use are still being determined.

Our history in working to support decisions and policies in telemedicine service scientifically started in 2017, with the project named 'TeleOftalmo,' which consists of a telemedicine service for not complex ophthalmologic issues, such as measuring the eyeglass parameters and making it arrive at patient's home. The structure was based on a physical clinic with ophthalmologists based in Porto Alegre, who executed the consultation online for patients who physically attended the offices in 7 different small cities across the State, being received and prepared by nurses' technicians and nurses—the initiative aimed to accelerate the diagnosis process and unburden the specialized clinics.

TeleOftalmo started as a research project, and using a service experiment approach, we had to begin to follow the service and analyze data from the system to understand the consultations' behavior and determine the most effective way to structure it. For example, on average, the simple information of how long the consultation with the ophthalmologist will take and how long it will take for patients to get prepared at the offices by the technicians was yet to be discovered. Consequently, estimating the number of patients that could be assisted monthly or how much it would account for was not possible initially. However, we had a great new opportunity in this project: using data at the patient level from the telemedicine software to analyze these lengths of time and resource consumption data. For the first time, it will be possible to automate the data input to estimate individual costs.

The project allowed us to discover two essential contributions to the health system:

As with most innovation processes, Telemedicine services are also exposed to a maturity learning curve. Our first findings demonstrated that it was necessary for 3-4 months for the service to achieve a stable balance of required resources and 6-7 months to achieve the expected volume of consultations and, consequently, the target costs. The chart below was adapted from one of the study papers published and demonstrates this maturity curve on the cost per consultation unit.[19] During the first months, it was being discovered the service behavior and adjusted the level of resources required for each activity. From December to April, the services were being disseminated across society, and the volume of consultations increased.

Costs per consultation curve.

Souce: adapted from Zanotto et. Al (2019) 19

The telemedicine service, in this case, resulted in the same perception of service quality from the patient's perspective and can be cost-saving to the system under a strong leadership and data-based management process. The radar chart below is adapted from the second research article published on this project. It is possible to see that the perception of patients' quality of life under a face-to-face consultation and those under the telemedicine services is equivalent. In contrast, the normalized cost information for a scenario of balanced service is lower on the telemedicine strategy. Measuring this is how it is possible to not only emphasize the impact of telemedicine but justify with data the potential impact of adopting telemedicine services in the history of increasing access to specialized care services.[20]

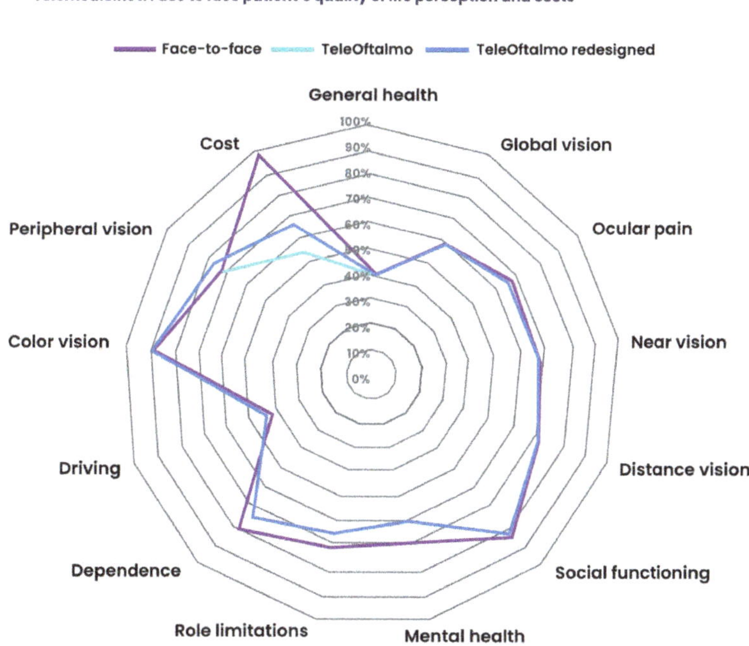

Source: adapted from Etges et. Al (2020) [20]

PART B

If the bottleneck is the data collection process, how can the available technology minimize it? The answer to that is what health tech companies are starting to address. Hospitals and health organizations' challenges in structuring their processes based on care pathways for specific clinical conditions also affect how the systems are coded. The previous chapter of this book shared an overview of the non-alignment across how services are paid and what is expected from effective health services. As most payments are based on volume and procedures, the traditional digital systems used by thousands of hospitals worldwide are much more driven to monitor procedures than patients' care pathways. However, once histories of projects achieving better outcomes by centering care processes and measuring patients' outcomes start to be known, changing the information technology systems structures becomes a requirement of organizations that put value transformation on their strategies. As a market answer to that, new chapters on the health tech industry have been written with robust and scalable solutions that can serve as turning points in patient-level outcomes and cost measurement.

During the TDABC Consortium Meeting in Lisbon, two software companies, one from the US (Avant-garde Health) and another from Portugal (Prologica), that work with the value-based healthcare concept motivated the members by having already solutions to share. From the meeting day to now, both registered steps on the path to share how they are making history in cost assessment in the healthcare field.

In the US, several hospitals are accounting for technologies that automate all the patients' time stamps and supply data collection, allowing them to execute microcosting analysis, including data from thousands of individuals, much faster. The orthopedics field concentrates most of the examples, and recently, it was possible to publish one of the first multicenter studies with accurate cost information of arthroscopic rotator cuff repair from US hospitals. In addition to reporting the actual cost, which is usually normalized to avoid the organization's exposition, the volume of cases the study included allowed us to measure the financial impact of the variability on the surgical path across the hospitals and the supply cost acquisition. Turning public this information through scientific papers elucidates the importance of using those data to renegotiate prices and manage in-hospital processes.[21]

By making it feasible to include data from thousands of cases quickly, the incorporation of software on the cost assessment initiatives breaks the bottleneck of microcosting studies that affirm 'Although microcosting is the gold standard method to evaluate costs in healthcare, it can not be scaled or generalized for populations perspectives and is, in general, only applied in small samples. This review paper published on Frontiers in Pharmacology [22] demonstrates that projects supported by technology on data collection include more than 1000 patients as samples and are being developed in a shorter period than the purely manually based one.

This is an important landmark for scientists, but the most crucial contribution is for healthcare executives.

The study consolidates the answers to all the CEOs and CFOs who ask us, "How does TDABC, supported by technology to automate cost analysis, result in cost savings? How much does it impact?" By developing this review, we demonstrated that technological advances contribute to delivering more precise measures to identify cost-saving opportunities, mainly based on supply variabilities, and accelerate redefining payment agreements with suppliers and healthcare payers.

So, why is it more disseminated in the US than in other countries?

Answering this point will make us come back to the reimbursement issue. In the US, The Center of Medicare & Medicaid Services (CMS) and private insurers are quickly expanding the use of outcomes-based bundle agreements considering complete care cycles. This means that hospitals and clinics are paid for delivering effective patient care, including the amount to be paid for supply items, professional services, hospital structure, etc. In 2023, the NEJM Catalyst consolidated the history of 10 years of CMS bundle payments, reporting successes and challenges of more than 50 programs implemented at the time by the State.[23] With this expressive presence of those agreements, several hospitals have modified their processes to deliver effective care along with the entire care pathway and consider all necessary resources. Using the new cost assessment technologies described, hospitals have easy access to variabilities in supply acquisition costs, for example, and use this information to renegotiate agreements with the suppliers, contributing to establishing a more homogeneous and sustainable system. Taking Brazil as an example to answer why it is not being scaled across other countries, by having most of the reimbursment system paying standardized fees by procedures, variabilities in supply acquisition costs do not affect the financial sustainability of hospitals directly because, in general, it is transmitted to payers, that as final consequence increment the insurance monthly payment of each individual. In other words, in the end, the variability in acquisition costs contributes to medical inflation. Still, it does not pressure hospitals to renegotiate prices with suppliers, and the society is who pays more for receiving the same.

This exemplification clarifies how the available technology and science about the impact of transforming payments can contribute significantly to establishing more effective healthcare systems. However, it will only be achieved and become a landmark in history if it is followed by strong leadership in defining and executing value-based health policies.

The Portuguese company's history is slightly different and has achieved other organizational and system implications. Just after the Consortium meeting, Anne Gebeulle, Prologica's CEO, invited me to collaborate on the challenge of developing a hospital system based on TDABC, the complete cost accounting system. Although I had already created several research projects, this was the opportunity to try everything we were building and advancing as scientists in a real-world context. Our final delivery will be the software implemented and attended, in addition to the cost management requests and the accountability requirements. At the same time, my curiosity and wish to try to make it surfaced, and I immediately confirmed that I was with her on that.

We joined a new team composed of software engineers, health economists, accountants, and cost managers, and we started to follow the TDABC steps. Let's stop quickly on that: **It does not matter the size of the challenge; when we have a solid, scientifically validated methodology, by following it, the expected results will be achieved.** And we did exactly that. In a few months, we were with the care pathways mapped and starting to define the software rules based on the TDABC equations. In 2022, the Portuguese hospital was already using the software, and at the end of 2023, the hospital's CEO received a national Premio award in Portugal for the project.

Unlike the US solution, this software allows for increased internal data accuracy rather than external benchmark analyses. From the angle of hospital managers, it can support a more precise management process of resource consumption per patient inside the organization. Variability analyses can be done at an organizational level, which means comparing the mean length of time or supply consumption between surgeons of the orthopedic service but not across organizations. In the future, if more hospitals start to incorporate the solution, it will be possible to create a benchmark culture and identify the services registering more effective care per patient treated.

The experience absorbed with this project amplified the opportunities to develop patient-centered digital solutions with other goals, which are much more driven for system implications under a national project involving several reference centers. In 2024, the software advances are in the pilot phase of version 2: it is being coded a specific platform to follow outcomes and cost data for bariatric and cataract surgery care pathways over the complete cycle of care, which means 2 years for the bariatric, for example. Achieving success on the pilot project will represent a landmark in Portuguese Health Tech development and system jump to manage care pathways based on real-world data.

However, in this case, the history is not finished yet, but we see extremely positive perspectives so far. It is expected that in a few months, Portuguese hospitals will be able to incorporate a platform that allows for identifying benchmarks of care at a national level, which has direct implications for the healthcare system and patients. Achieving those results of patients having access to quality-of-care information before getting into a health center means providing accurate data to society and having the capability to decide together with clinicians where and why a few centers may concentrate more volume than others. Ultimately, it means providing data to increase the trust of all stakeholders in the healthcare system.

From technology to health policies

The histories reported exemplify why and how technology is a strong element in transforming the healthcare system from procedure and volume for the population to individualized care. It is already feasible to generate real-time data that provide the integrated journey of each individual, which contributes to the clinician's work and the system's transparency; consequently, it increases trust across the system chain. Although we recognize its importance, it is also paramount not to put it in front of the medical function to provide the medical service. Technology may serve as a 'best friend' or a great ally, but it never serves as the clinician's voice or the healthcare system's accountability.

The advances worldwide demonstrate that health leaders and policymakers might open their eyes and invest in structuring strategies that make these 'best friends' available to providers and health workers, increasing value in health by positively impacting healthcare services access, equity, and quality. Technology alone cannot change history, but it is a consensus that the leaders of society need and can use technology and real-world data as assets to plan, structure, and deliver health services that address societal needs. The effectiveness of this needs to deal with balancing risks on data protection and, mainly, with the risk of losing the healthcare system's purpose. It is necessary to keep the focus on investments in the sector to be translated into increases in population health with financial accountability metrics, and not only in other angles of measuring impact that do not consider health outcomes.

Our next chapter includes a history of how the risk management field can be a strong ally on this journey.

Risk management and governance in healthcare histories

What is risk in healthcare?

What is risk in healthcare? I confess that this question motivated me to do my Ph.D thesis. Healthcare is exposed to several downsides and upside risks, which can be internal or external events that affect the institutional capacities to deliver healthcare services with quality, safety, and financial sustainability. A sentinel event, such as a baby death or an active shooter attack, a risk that can cause damage to the institution, as well, the establishment of a measured payment agreement for a specific clinical condition, as well as automation of clinical data collection and facilitate the clinician's communication is an opportunity that can be achieved by taking the risk to digitalize a health center.

Although our research group has published several papers on this topic, including a risk inventory in 2018 [24], the history of this is much more connected to how we have learned during the last years that risk management is an essential element in moving healthcare systems to value.

Why does managing risks in healthcare matter to increase value in health?

The previous chapters shared several examples of how strong and gritty leadership with purpose, accurate data, and scientifically validated methods successfully guides policymakers in dealing with healthcare system failure. However, it also changes how all the stakeholders, including the general society, participate in this process and the healthcare system. No stakeholder will change their process, actions, behaviors, or culture if this change does not bring a potentially positive opportunity to him: Hospitals will accept changing agreements with payers (and vice-versa) if they identify that it can be sustainable, and mainly if it contributes to balancing risks between them and does not transfer more risk to only one part; Patients will be more likely to change behaviors if they understand and have access to the real implications for their health in the short and long term, including, for example, the opportunity to receive discounts on monthly fees by adopting healthier habits. Otherwise, people and companies will keep processes and habits as they have. Transparently demonstrating the positive implications and the effort to make them happen is part of the changing process, which depends on a decision-making practice exposed to risks. In this process, people must decide about the risks they will accept, mitigate, or avoid.

So, what is the risk of doing nothing to change healthcare systems?

First: the history of health policy and economics studies shows the tendency to increase healthcare expenses annually without improving populations' health indicators. Doing nothing is to keep watching this tendency until it collapses, as we were exposed to during the COVID-19 pandemic.

Second: Technology scalability in the healthcare business is highly accelerated. Although this means innovation and opportunities to make it feasible to guarantee a better quality of life for people with different clinical conditions, it also demands more effort from policymakers to maintain system sustainability.

Third: With the data access explosion, not defining regulations for using it ethically can result in a breach of fake news and non-compliance actions, worsening the system's capability to deliver care.

Fourth: we will keep watching a system that is oriented to deliver and pay for services but not worried and oriented to provide health care. The system will keep paying for healthcare rather than for health.

Assume the challenge of conducting strategic transformations aimed at creating more valuable systems is how this level of risk exposure can be mitigated, but its effectiveness requires balancing the risks across all the stakeholders.

By researching risk management in healthcare, I had the opportunity to interview dozens of chief risk officers from Brazilian and US hospitals. It happened in 2017. At the time, in the US, the digitalization of health was happening, and innovative payment agreements were a tendency, in addition to having groups of health centers with several specialized units geographically distributed. While in Brazil, the context was a few years behind, and the most recognized hospitals were still concentrated in a huge unit, payments were primarily based on fee-for-service agreements, and digitalization of health was in discussion but starting to happen slowly. Independently, the structuring of risk units aimed to evaluate the business risks was valued in both countries, with different maturities. The US risk managers were already assuming the requirement for change, putting the risk of doing nothing with the strategy of measuring data and payment as high, while the Brazilians were still trying to define their space as more strategic than the clinical risk managers, who for years worked pretty close to the honored field of quality and safety.

Independently of those differences in maturity, by consolidating the main risks that the literature and the chief risk officers from both countries point out at the time, it was possible to identify Cyber security Organizational Culture, Sentinel Events, Ethical use of Electronic Health Records, and Physician wellness as the top 5 risks, which means that more than 90% of people interviewed agreed that those are extremely important enterprise risks as show the Figure above adapted from the original article.

Main enterprise risks that healthcare organizations are exposed to

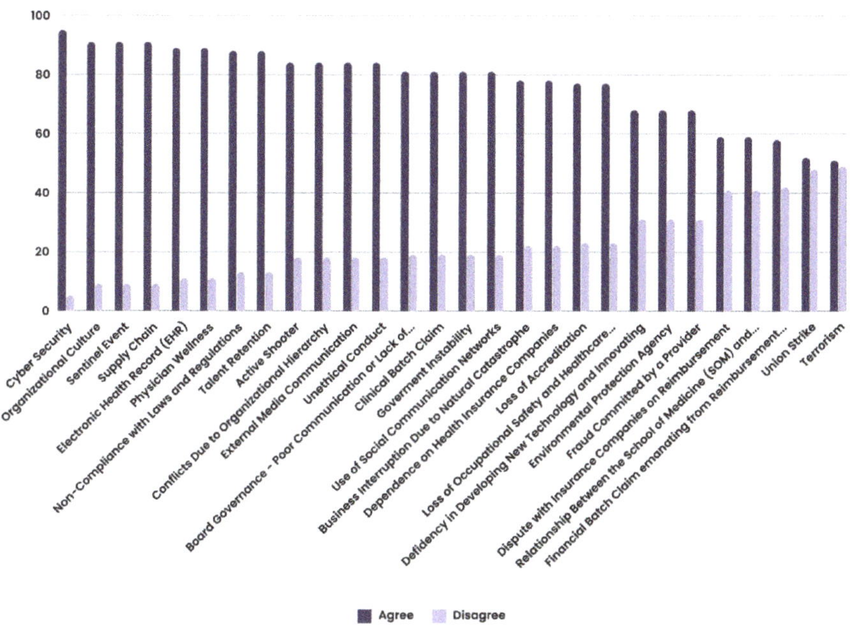

Source: Adapted from Etges et al. (2018)[24]

Seven years after the interviews, in 2024, and after all the learning from the pandemic and the modifications we observe in how organizations are structured, these top 5 risks still make sense and concentrate massive efforts from chief risk officers. As shared in the first two chapters of this book, the healthcare system has been submitted during the last few years to the highest investments in data protection, standardization, and digitalization. All those changes in payment and monitoring, moving from a volume to a populational-based perspective, involve significant cultural changes, maximizing patients' quality and safety with financial accountability. The wrong side of history is that we have not done a great job of creating strong structures to manage those risks. Let me point out a few reasons for the data protection and the organizational cultural risks.

Managing risks of data protection and digitalization health

The risk management goal for data protection is to identify the balance between protecting the individual and using real-world data to build a more reliable system. However, in practice, this can be highly complex and open space for a 'political war', and consequently, delay in implementing structural changes in healthcare systems if rigorous regulations are not established soon. Modifying the payment agreements, for example, depends on data sharing among providers and payers, respecting all the compliance required. At the same time, in Brazil, we still have problems using real-world data for research objectives, making the path a long journey. In a recent research project to provide cost information on cardiac surgery, for example, we could not have access to electronic medical record data of more than 40 patients from a public hospital because the surgeries had happened before the hospital implemented the system for patients authorized to be invited for research.

Other countries around the globe have worked on establishing clear laws and internal policies to mitigate data protection risk and change this history. The European Union, for example, in early 2024, launched the 'European Health Data Space – EHDS' (https://health.ec.europa.eu/ehealth-digital-health-and-care/european-health-data-space_en) with the aim of:

- empowering individuals to take control of their data and facilitate the exchange of data for the delivery of healthcare across the EU;

- foster a genuine single market for electronic health record systems; and

- provide a consistent, trustworthy, and efficient system for reusing health data for research, innovation, policy-making, and regulatory activities.

Once the data is anonymized following the European General Data Protection Law, it can be considered for the EHDS, which allows organizations and researchers to use it to develop patient-centered solutions and scientific answers based on real-world data. A similar flow for data use happens in the US. The FDA makes millions of anonymized data available for companies and researchers, contributing to the country's several registers of massive datasets. In addition to the federal initiatives, the US accounts for public datasets from organizations that structure it for scientific purposes; one of the most famous is the MIMIC [25], which contains data from patients hospitalized at the Beth Israel Deaconess Medical Center. By having access to these vast and reliable datasets, European countries and the US have assumed leadership in developing scientific advances for society based on real-world data and, consequently, opened the door for building healthcare histories based on real human histories.

The advances in regulations to make those datasets publicly available are elemental for making it feasible to explore the power of data to increase value in the healthcare system. The acceleration in how it has become available around the globe brings us hope on the journey to create histories of healthcare systems based on real-world data, mitigating the risk of data protection.

Managing risks of cultural transformations in health organizations

As humans, we are naturally afraid of changes. We are more likely to accept and adapt, but changes bring uncertainty, doubt, and stress. At the same time, innovating with success involves changing how people solve routine problems, causing the lower stress of change that is possible. One of the usual trade-offs of innovation processes is to balance the risk of causing too much stress on innovating and avoiding innovative transformations and dying as a business because people choose to change to identify opportunities to adopt a new way to do something; in general, something that is not well solved. Simple things, such as Uber and Airbnb, are excellent examples of that. A few years ago, it would have seemed absurd to travel around the world renting apartments (not hotels) for 1 or 2 nights or to get in the car of a strange you order by an app to go to a destination. Today, it is strange to be in a city where you only have taxis or public transportation to travel. As citizens, we accept these new business models as the latest solutions, while we avoid others by seeing that they can cause too many changes in a short time, such as the Cruise and the automated Taxi tested in 2023.

Why?

Airbnb or Uber introduced innovative business models and solutions to the market that contributed to solving people's routine problems with comprehensive, not complex, changes in human behavior. While getting in a car without a human driver can be too much to introduce to society. This is to identify the balance between the necessity for innovation and the level of changes internal teams can accept, which can vary from one organization to another and is associated with organizational risk fitness. What happens in healthcare is that most organizations are traditionally structured in a conservative way; the innovation and risk fitness cause stress, uncertainty, fear, etc.

The leadership challenge to manage those feelings is to discover how to balance the team fitness for the introduction of innovative processes, agreements, and manners of measuring and communicating. Since the first histories shared in this book, gritty leadership has been pointed out as a key factor in the healthcare systems and organizations' strategic implementation cases. It is not different when the topic is to organize teams to work in a much more integrated approach. However, assuming the risk of innovating how teams and processes are implemented is necessary.

In redesigning healthcare services, it is commonplace to identify activities that nurses can assume instead of clinicians, contributing to decreasing costs and increasing access to physicians. From this angle, it is a win-win identification. The angle of discussing with clinicians that they need to change their routines and share more activities with nurses can become a problem. Mitigating the risk of making this simple initiative become a negative issue on the team is a leadership role and involves having effective communication capabilities. Each day, it is strictly aligned with having accurate data and using it to quantify the history of storytelling for communicating.

Effective Communication as a successful key to governance

During the development process of the first cost assessment project designed to evaluate the cost of doing a bone marrow transplant in Brazil[26], it was measured that the care unit nurse leader spent more than 80% of her time doing administrative tasks instead of direct care activities with patients. At the same time, the nurse team registered many overtime rates monthly, resulting in more expenses, provider burnout, and, in the case of a bone marrow transplant, a higher exposure to infections. Previously to the project, it was a perception from the nurse team, but it has never been measured. With the metrics on hand, we reported what was happening to the board, suggesting reallocating the nursing team and hiring an administrative staff to support them. By bringing the nurse leader closer to patients, it will be possible to reduce the overtime rate and the expenses with the new professional will account for a lower impact than paying for nurses' overhead. In other words, changing the allocation and hiring someone else specific for administrative tasks was a cost-saving strategy and changed the history of overhead and correlated problems.

Two facts were fundamental to this process: (i) communicating the problem based on data to the board, who decides, and (ii) having the nurse and the clinical leadership support the analysis and the request from the beginning. Nothing would have advanced or been done without their leadership and internal support based on data.

More recently, in developing projects to implement integrated practical units for cardiovascular disease prevention and asthma, one more time can be mentioned: effective communication with strong leadership to redesign care services. In those cases, the cultural and process modifications were not restricted to only one organization but involved providers, payers, the pharmaceutical industry, and patients. It involves creating a sense of moving strategies from an organizational to regional responsibility, and making it happen requires integrating all the stakeholders from the early stage. By doing that, on both cases and care pathways, cardiovascular disease prevention, and asthma, there is a chance of changing how the Brazilian population will access specialized care, expecting to register fewer strokes, heart attacks, and asthma crises across the country.

One more time, we are using healthcare strategy science to make history in creating a better healthcare system every day.

Creating a culture of valuable histories in healthcare organizations

Several value-oriented initiatives are happening, and histories are being consolidated with lessons learned for the next ones that start. However, it is notable that, at a system level, there is a lot to be done, and we still have huge variability in how a few countries are more or less structured to make the required transformations in the healthcare system aiming to make it more populational based and less volume based. Reducing inequity, facilitating access, reducing waste, being precise in defining health technology policies and reimbursement strategies... the list of challenges is long. Although they have been worked on and researched daily, there are no simple and unique answers to address each.

Education investment is a trigger for creating more evidence-based and less politically influenced systems.

One reason that is already a consensus for that is the lack of education on those topics we see; in simple words, the healthcare system concentrates on average 10% of the gross domestic product (GDP) of countries, and healthcare professionals are not submitted to at least one discipline of finance, economy, management at most of the under graduations courses around the world. On the other hand, most business and economy courses bring many more learning opportunities for finance, industrial, and technology markets than the healthcare sector. Consequently, it is not rare to see in front of prominent health organizations or in the position of policymakers who were not strongly prepared over their academic journey to deal with the defiant and extremely important to society's progress in the healthcare sector. At the same time, society needs fast answers, positions, and decisions from them as soon as possible. In an environment where there is a need for educational dissemination, the freedom of companies and leaders to innovate and contribute faster to introducing solutions is affected, and they face barriers to being disseminated.

Let's come back to the telemedicine example shared previously in this book. The scientific analysis demonstrated that the service could be cost-saving, is well accepted by patients, and can accelerate access to the healthcare system. It was published, making the information available to the public, but the initiative was not multiplied across the country or amplified. Part of the reason is the decision-maker's lack of comprehension of the contribution of those services, which resulted in political influences on deciding about the amplification of the project. The only way to mitigate the negative impact of political influences not based on evidence and history is by disseminating a higher educational level among young people who will be future leaders soon. This is undoubtedly a worry we need to think about as people working for a sector that strongly impacts people's lives, and it is already a concern in the risk assessment market.

I am a millennium. I remember today the surprise I got when attending the American Society of Risk Management in Healthcare Conference in 2017 in Seattle to present results from my Ph.D thesis by hearing several sessions discussing the impact of the millennium generation arriving at leadership positions in healthcare companies. The main concern that the speakers raised was the commitment that this generation will continue structuring long-term projects with such an impact on society and that this generation will be strongly prepared and educated for the multidisciplinary environment of the healthcare sector. At the same time, it is a worry; it also pressures people who work in education to promote manners to involve the new generations in educational journeys that encourage the creation of grit, which we already know is necessary to create successful histories. One more time, leaders who follow validated science and the creation of effective communication with different audiences are fundamental elements. As educators, leaders, policymakers, and entrepreneurs, we must identify "How" to make it happen.

One inspirable example was publicly shared in 2024 in the article reporting the Mass General Brigham Hospital's history of measuring Patient Reported Outcomes since 2012, which resulted in a long list of lessons and learnings concentrated on the piece.[27] With millions of data already collected and thousands of people involved, one of the most impactful parts is the creation of the "Patient-Reported Outcomes, Value, and Experience (PROVE) Center". The PROVE aims to use a huge dataset with real-world data from patients' perspectives to generate evidence-based science that guides innovation in healthcare delivery. For example, measuring how socio-determinants of health (SDOH) impact the effectiveness of health technologies and identifying variabilities can be used to modify its use guidelines. It is how to create continuous learning and applied culture using PROMs data to develop a valuable healthcare system based on science.

For managers, clinicians, and health leaders who already have access to those datasets, it is a light of inspiration about how gold real-world data is already available and can be used for discovering potential landmarks for improving the healthcare system, organizations, and the most important part, individuals' health. It is evident from the history reported that it is feasible, but it requires investments in people with research, innovation, and technology backgrounds and in cultivating the learning cycle in this field with the new generations. This is an excellent example of converting investments in science into applied solutions with societal impact that can be followed by any organization around the world aiming to design, implement, and keep data-driven healthcare systems.

Real-world evidence and a new era in developing health policy

One of the most impactful aspects behind using real-world data and evidence in healthcare is the opportunity to provide high-quality and real-time data to guide more assertive decisions with fewer political influences. Data are data, and it always has something to say, allowing us to quantify histories. We cannot fight against data; but we can act and do something to make the data tell the history we wish. The world already has a vast capability to digitalize people's lives, from wearables to hospital records. The technology to make the data available is not the problem; having access to it, respecting compliance aspects, and, most importantly, having the capabilities to make the data say something are the challenges.

The challenge involves keeping the healthcare sector attractive for tech companies and investors and the government's commitment to regulating the industry for using data safely and ethically. The implications of joining academic, private, and public investments on developing innovative solutions and discoveries based on science are exponential. Just a few years after the Apple Watch with cardio functionalities launched, in 2018, for example, a union from Stanford University and Apple made it feasible to join more than 400,000 individuals in 9 months in one of the first clinical trials 100% digital to confirm if the wearable was able to detect atrial fibrillation.[28] In the history of this study, it is interesting to highlight that the University involvement had a crucial role in addition to academic knowledge: it served as the neutral field to guarantee access to data without breaking the US regulations about using wearable data for research purposes. It differs from the several microcosting projects we have done and reported previously. It is clear and transparent that the pharma companies are interested in the cost information to submit new technologies for incorporation processes but cannot access the granular cost data required to develop accurate studies by themselves. The neutral field that should permanently be established on scientific groups is extremely important to be kept in the Era of using real-world data to generate real-world evidence that can contribute to creating a history of a more patient-centered and value-oriented health care system.

Creating culture by involving people with the purpose of creating more effective healthcare systems

Medical science is always being updated, and the technological advances in using real-world data also reduce the time required to introduce new products, methods, and processes. In this context, keeping multi-disciplinary teams continually educated and updated is a challenge that needs to be assumed by the academic and non-academic entities. It put on the table the challenge of providing access to technologies and guaranteeing that the teams' background and expertise are at the level required to use the technologies available better. In countries such as Brazil, which is exposed to a vast heterogeneity in people's education and socio-determinants of health, making it at a system level is furthermore defiant but not impossible. The critical point in making content and innovation achieve a large group of different people is to make it easy to access and understand.

With these simple requirements in mind, it was born in 2019 with a national project in Brazil named "Care Pathways in the National Public Healthcare System in Brazil." Having on its ideation process an extremely gritty Professor from the Epidemiology School of the South of Brazil who served as secretary at the municipality and federal level, the project had the goal to define care pathways based on the most updated guidelines and evidence, respecting the technologies available in Brazil; educate health professionals, managers and the society across the country; disseminate it is an easy and friendly platform. The objectives posted already elucidate the size of the challenge. However, the purpose of facilitating the dissemination of education with direct implications for the population health in our country moved people to find resources and make it happen in 18 months.

The impact of the initiative in a continental middle-income country contributed to the project receiving funding from the Pan-American Health Organization (OPAS), and our research group was responsible for coordinating the project for 22 care pathways. A team composed of epidemiologists, nurses with experience in health economics, and engineers was structured, and for each clinical care pathway, experts and medical societies were interviewed. As soon as the content for a specific care pathway was elaborated, it was submitted for validation by the Ministry of Health. This process guaranteed the first objective of the project of "defining care pathways based on the most updated guidelines and evidence, respecting the technologies available in Brazil," but making it easy to assess required an additional strategy.

After a few meetings with the leaders involved in this project, it was a consensus that the best strategy to make the care pathways content available for a large scale and different audience would be having the care pathways digitalized on a web page with the content prepared with 3 different approaches: for health professionals, managers, and patients. A software development company was hired to work on the project. Over 18 months, the process of developing content, validating, and coding it on a web platform was followed, and the product can be accessed online (www.linhasdecuidado.saude.gov.br).

Although the product generated is essential to disseminating education across the country, this project was also a landmark on the value of structuring and standardizing, considering the best evidence, and how to deliver care for each specific care pathway in a healthcare system. After its launching, several initiatives oriented to structure care pathways emerged in the private and public sectors, and the theme has won a strong space each year. It contributes to change in the Brazilian history of structuring care pathways to deliver more effective care to society and increase population access to reliable health content.

By disseminating standardized clinical care pathways, it is also possible to start strategies for digitalizing it. Several companies offering those services have been introduced to the market, the oncological field being the one with more examples. Among the characteristics of those solutions is the report of patient outcomes and symptoms and the establishment of a proactive service to monitor patients and act by identifying any signs of worsening in the health status.

The scientific results evaluating these initiatives already suggest how they can be impactful. In Belgium, for example, implementing a digital care pathway for lung cancer patients was compared with the traditional care model. [29] Ever 6 weeks, patients reported outcomes using an app and the nursing team at the hospital monitored the answers. If something varies from the previous report, the team proactively contacts patients and guides them about what should be done. The project decreased mortality, emergency visits, and outpatient consultations for the patients under the digital care pathway. They were also allowed to demonstrate the variability in the perception of patients and clinicians about their health status, as exhibited in the figure below.

Patients' perception x clinicians' perception

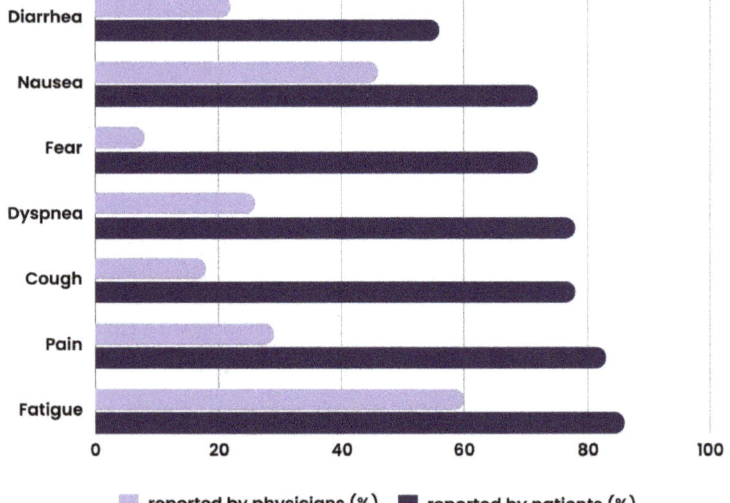

Source: adapted from Demedts et al. (2021) [29]

By sharing the results of successful cases such as the one from Belgium, more people will understand how; by creating a culture of measuring the patients' perspectives and proactively acting according to the most evidence available, it is possible to change the natural history of disease and promote health by also engaging people in this purpose. This case joins the dissemination of education, technology investment, patient engagement, and driving care pathways to value.

The several histories generated on accurate cost assessment also have, as its start, moments of sharing achievements with the right people to awaken them to the cause of worry about the cost information. When the heart transplant study was finished, the cardiologist leading the clinical aspect of the project invited all the professors behind transplant programs at the academic hospital to a meeting. At the moment, I could not imagine what this would mean to the history of microcosting studies in Brazil and, consequently, my history in this field. My role on this day was to present the heart transplant cost study to the group. Bingo!!! For the first time, a group of almost 15 senior Professors was introduced to the TDABC method and its implications in providing good quality cost data and, most importantly, how this information could guide more assertive health policies. At the same time, this group of experts is recognized as senior leaders in their clinical fields. Still, their curriculums did not introduce education on health economics methods and their importance to society. Having contact with the power of using that associated with their current level of knowledge on the clinical aspect makes them identify the value of doing this kind of research. After this meeting, we started to receive several master's and Ph.D. students asking for our support to serve as second supervisors on their academic projects, supervised by one of the professors at the meeting with us.

Looking back, it is clear how, by communicating and educating the right leaders about the opportunities of adding economic analysis to clinical research protocols, a culture of measuring and developing projects based on value-based healthcare principles started to be created. This meeting happened in 2018, and during the last few years, the scale of projects and initiatives in this field has won considerable space at organizational and system levels. As scientists behind several applied projects, we have also assumed the responsibility of getting the right people involved in this cause. By offering courses for companies and through medical societies, people in leadership positions get educated, and we can see that each year, the culture of value in health is growing and influencing the execution of projects.

The high level of education on health policy, strategy, and value being disseminated among people who make history in healthcare is a key element for changing cultures and systems and getting closer to the history we would like to tell about health systems in 10 years.

What is the history we wish to tell in 10 years?

Before answering this question, let's explore what being a good and sustainable country means. Independently of political orientations, healthcare is always a state priority, and this will never change. What policymakers can avoid by following scientific evidence is making healthcare not a political issue but always a priority policy for society. The advances in the capability to generate evidence and directions about the best healthcare practices advanced fast during the last decades, making the sector concentrate most of the scientific advances available. Still, the velocity with which leaders can incorporate those advances into the system has not followed the same rhythm. In this context, our answer to the history we want to tell in 10 years is associated with identifying how to accelerate the process of changing organizational and system cultures and strategies for a much more integrated, population-based, patient-centered, and real-world data-driven, instead of volume-based, process-centered and non-data-driven healthcare system. Frameworks, such as the LEADER previously explored in this book and the Value Agenda introduced by Prof Porter with the concept of value, if followed by strong and gritty leaders, can help organize this process and guide policymakers.

For Leadership and Care Integration, it is expected to account for histories as the Spanish are creating with the HOPE project, and the Portuguese are structuring for bariatric surgery, for example. In both cases, projects are being planned and invested at a strategic institutional or system level, executed based on scientific evidence, centered on patient's needs, educating all professionals involved, and using accurate data to engage all the stakeholders, including patients.

We wish to see inspiring leaders who promote initiatives like those for several clinical conditions. This would allow us to tell the complete history of the impact that is causing on population health and potentially consolidate best practices for implementing and reimbursing the most effective clinical protocols for every healthcare system.

Changes in how services are delivered, and systems are structured need effective agreements. In this field, several examples of histories are emerging worldwide. Each manager's role is to evaluate the one that fits each context and clinical condition. While rare diseases can be almost the perfect scenario for using risk-sharing agreements, chronic disease can account for hybrid models, with the standard routine services being paid by service with a proportion of bonification due to achieving expected outcomes. Significant outcomes have real implications for population health, not only confirming service delivery to society. It means analyzing the proportion of women with breast cancer suspect that confirmed diagnosis and, if necessary, started the treatment in a short period and not only evaluating the proportion of women doing the mammogram.

We wish to see more agreements based on outcomes that matter to patients, with financial accountability and long-term sustainability models for payers, suppliers, and providers.

Measuring accurate data is each day more a requirement for any advance in the healthcare sector, which, in its essence, is a scientific-based market. Those who do not measure do not have sustained argumentation and evidence to tell a good history or to produce science. Investing in technology capability to make data available for patients, providers, payers, and policymakers, respecting the required compliance, is almost investing in gold in the current context. The expectations about the acceleration of using real-world data and following patients include precisely identifying people's habits and technologies, resulting in better health, and identifying what really matters to each individual after a medical procedure to evaluate his health status. While we see exponential advances in using artificial intelligence to solve societal problems, if we do not have good data, its usability is limited and can be dangerous to the population's health. The MIMIC dataset and the new efforts observed in Europe after the law update in 2024 are landmarks of how investing in making high-quality data available to the general market and society provides answers to drive valuable projects to increase population health.

We wish to have more health technology decisions based on data, people educated and engaged in self-care based on data, value-based agreements based on data, and data serving as a strong subside for health policy decisions taken by humans, guaranteeing the incorporation of local wisdom in each step advanced. We wish to have data being used and valued as the primary source for good answers for population health, as gold is used to balance economies anywhere.

Risks are at the heart of the healthcare sector; every day inside a hospital can be a surprise box in a way that only by establishing effective models to manage processes and risks is it possible to keep excellence in healthcare delivery. This is the core concept of most accreditation programs available, such as Joint Commission International (JCI), that help organizations improve performance and outcomes. Being a purist, clinical risk management is the origin of quality and safety histories in healthcare. In the business sustainability perspective, mitigating the concentration of risks at only one stakeholder is how innovative business models are introduced, resulting in win-win impacts, i.e., impacting people's access to the healthcare system and balancing costs and profits across payers, providers, and suppliers.

We wish to see a risk mitigation culture across all the stakeholders from the healthcare chain that keeps the system's focus on delivering health to society. Establishing agreements defining and sharing risks can potentially increase the chances of creating a health system that is more fair, valuable to all stakeholders, and focused on population needs.

By concisely evaluating the impact of scientific strategies tested and implemented in the healthcare sector, we wish to use science to reduce healthcare suffering and create everyday chapters of the history of a system driven by increasing population health with financial accountability.

References

1. Duckworth A. *Grit: The Power of Passion and Perseverance.* Vol 234. Scribner New York, NY; 2016.

2. Porter ME. What is value in health care. *N Engl J Med.* 2010;363(26):2477-2481.

3. Porter ME, Teisberg EO. *Redefining Health Care: Creating Value-Based Competition on Results.* Harvard Business Press; 2006.

4. da Silva Etges APB, Polanczyk CA, Nabi J. Revitalizing Stroke Care: The LEADER Strategy for Sustainable Transformation in Health Care Delivery. *Stroke.*

5. Etges APB da S, Lara LR de, Sapper SL, et al. Redesign of radiotherapy for prostate cancer: a proposal for universal healthcare systems. *J Comp Eff Res.* 0(0):e230023. doi:10.57264/cer-2023-0023

6. Etges APB da S, Marcolino MAZ, Ogliari LA, et al. Moving the Brazilian ischaemic stroke pathway to a value-based care: introduction of a risk-adjusted cost estimate model for stroke treatment. *Health Policy Plan.* 2022;37(9):1098-1106.

7. da Silva Etges APB, Nabi J, Geubelle A, Martins SO, Polanczyk CA. Analytical Solutions to Support Value-based Health Care: The Ischemic Stroke Care Pathway Case. *NEJM Catal Innov Care Deliv.* 2022;3(1).

8. Caramés Sánchez C, Álvaro de la Parra JA, Dómine M, et al. The HOPE project: improving cancer patient experience and clinical outcomes through an integrated practice unit and digital transformation. *NEJM Catal Innov Care Deliv.* 2023;4(7):CAT-22.

9. Porter ME, Kaplan RS. How to pay for health care. *Harv Bus Rev.* 2016;94(7-8):88-98.

10. Tan SS, Rutten FFH, van Ineveld BM, Redekop WK, Hakkaart-van Roijen L. Comparing methodologies for the cost estimation of hospital services. *Eur J Health Econ HEPAC Health Econ Prev Care.* 2009;10(1):39-45. doi:10.1007/s10198-008-0101-x

11. Beck da Silva Etges AP, Urman RD, Geubelle A, Kaplan R, Polanczyk CA. Cost standard set program: moving forward to standardization of cost assessment based on clinical condition. Published online 2022.

12. Goldraich LA, Neyeloff JL, da Silva Etges APB, et al. Heart Transplantation Cost Composition in Brazil: A Patient-Level Microcosting Analysis and Comparison With International Data. *J Card Fail.* 2018;24(12):860-863.

13. Ghisleni EC, Astolfi VR, Zimmermann L, et al. Value-based health care in heart failure: Quality of life and cost analysis. *Clinics.* 2023;78:100294.

14. Etges APBS, Zanotto BS, Saccilotto IC, Ferrari RS, Satub ALP, Saute JAM, Marchesan T, Loze PM, Carlos NS, Polanczyk CA. Custos com os cuidados da atrofia muscular espinhal 5q (AME-5q) no Brasil. *Journal Brasileiro de Economica da Saúde.*

15. Schneider NB, Roos EC, Staub ALP, et al. Estimated costs for Duchenne muscular dystrophy care in Brazil. *Orphanet J Rare Dis.* 2023;18(1):1-8.

16. Etges A, Schneider N, Roos E, et al. EE63 Cost-Hemophilia Brazil. *Value Health*. 2023;26(6):S70-S71.

17. da Silva Etges APB, Cardoso RB, Marcolino MS, et al. The economic impact of COVID-19 treatment at a hospital-level: investment and financial registers of Brazilian hospitals. *J Health Econ Outcomes Res*. 2021;8(1):36.

18. Cardoso RB, Marcolino MAZ, Marcolino MS, et al. Comparison of COVID-19 hospitalization costs across care pathways: a patient-level time-driven activity-based costing analysis in a Brazilian hospital. *BMC Health Serv Res*. 2023;23(1):198.

19. Zanotto BS, Etges APB da S, Siqueira AC, et al. Economic Evaluation of a Telemedicine Service to expand Primary Health Care in Rio Grande do Sul: TeleOftalmo's microcosting analysis. *Ciênc Saúde Coletiva*. 2020;25:1349-1360.

20. da Silva Etges APB, Zanotto BS, Ruschel KB, et al. Telemedicine Versus Face-to-Face Care in Ophthalmology: Costs and Utility Measures in a Real-World Setting. *Value Health Reg Issues*. 2022;28:46-53.

21. Catherine J. Fedorka, Ana Paula Beck da Silva Etges, Matthew J. Best, et al. Defining the Cost of Arthroscopic Rotator Cuff Repair: A multicenter, time-driven activity-based costing and cost optimization investigation. Running-title: Multicenter TDABC study for Rotator Cuff Repair. *J Bone Jt Surg*. 2024;106.

22. Etges APBDS, Jones P, Liu H, Zhang X, Haas D. Improvements in technology and the expanding role of time-driven, activity-based costing to increase value in healthcare provider organizations: a literature review. *Front Pharmacol*. 2024;15:1345842.

23. Fowler E, Rudolph N, Davidson K, et al. Accelerating care delivery transformation—the CMS innovation center's

role in the next decade. *NEJM Catal Innov Care Deliv*. 2023;4(11):CAT-23.

24. da Silva Etges APB, Grenon V, Lu M, et al. Development of an enterprise risk inventory for healthcare. *BMC Health Serv Res*. 2018;18(1):578.

25. Johnson AE, Bulgarelli L, Shen L, et al. MIMIC-IV, a freely accessible electronic health record dataset. *Sci Data*. 2023;10(1):1.

26. da Silva Etges APB, Cruz LN, Notti RK, et al. An 8-step framework for implementing time-driven activity-based costing in healthcare studies. *Eur J Health Econ*. Published online July 8, 2019. doi:10.1007/s10198-019-01085-8

27. Liu JB, Kaplan RS, Bates DW, Edelen MO, Sisodia RC, Pusic AL. Mass General Brigham's Patient-Reported Outcomes Measurement System: A Decade of Learnings. *NEJM Catal Innov Care Deliv*. 2024;5(3):CAT-23.

28. Turakhia MP, Desai M, Hedlin H, et al. Rationale and design of a large-scale, app-based study to identify cardiac arrhythmias using a smartwatch: The Apple Heart Study. *Am Heart J*. 2019;207:66-75.

29. Demedts I, Himpe U, Bossuyt J, et al. Clinical implementation of value based healthcare: Impact on outcomes for lung cancer patients. *Lung Cancer*. 2021;162:90-95.

The author

Ana is passionate for inspiring people for scientific education and works for a more effective and sustainable healthcare system.

In addition to her position as Partner from PEV Healthcare Consulting, she serves as a Professor in the Graduate Program in Epidemiology at Universidade Federal do Rio Grande do Sul (UFRGS), at Hospital de Clínicas de Porto Alegre, and at Insper Healthcare Management MBA Program in Brazil, as a Senior Researcher at the National Institute for Health Technology Assessment (Brazil) and for Health Tech Companies in the United States. In all her affiliations, she has dedicated her career to increasing population health by turning healthcare data more transparent and implementing value-based principles in organizations and systems.

Ana has performed dozens of cost assessment and healthcare strategy research and consulting projects in Brazil, Portugal, and the USA. Because of that, she founded the TDABC in Healthcare Consortium in 2020, 2022 joined the ISPOR Task Force for Value-based Healthcare, and in 2024, joined the Future Leaders board of the International Network of Health Promoting Hospitals (HPH). In all her affiliations and collaborations, she is continually researching and working to engage more people in improving the efficiency of healthcare systems worldwide.

Ana is an Industrial engineer who graduated from Pontifícia Universidade Católica do Rio Grande do Sul (PUCRS). She concluded her MSc and Ph.D. in industrial engineering at UFRGS, having the Ph.D developed in collaboration with Stanford Medicine. She also completed her postdoctoral fellowship in Epidemiology at UFRGS, attended the VBHC Seminary at Harvard Business School in 2021, and is certified in Effective Writing for Health Care by Harvard Medical School (Class 2023).

Ana has an impressive portfolio as a consultant and researcher. She has penned more than 100 peer-reviewed scientific publications, all focusing on the intricate fields of healthcare strategy, value, leadership, policy, and economics.

Publique seu livro:

Conheça os livros da Editora Ases da Literatura em
www.asesdaliteratura.com